Interactive Bulletin Boards
SEPTEMBER TO JUNE

By
Judy Meagher
and
Joan Novelli

SCHOLASTIC
PROFESSIONAL BOOKS

NEW YORK • TORONTO • LONDON • AUCKLAND • SYDNEY

Daley

ACKNOWLEDGMENTS

Heartfelt thanks to Deborah Schecter, our editor at Scholastic Professional Books, for her artful guidance. Special thanks, also, to Paula Butterfield and the Bozeman School District; the teachers at Emily Dickinson School, Whittier School, Morning Star, and Heritage Christian School in Bozeman, Montana, for their help, support, and cooperation; and to all the children who brought the bulletin boards pictured in this book to life.

Project direction by Joan Novelli
Cover design by Jaime Lucero
Cover art by Jo Lynn Alcorn
Cover photographs by Judy Meagher
Interior design by Solutions by Design, Inc.
Interior photographs by Judy Meagher
Interior illustration by Paige Billin-Frye

ISBN 0-590-18739-2

Contents

From the Authors 4

Organizers at a Glance A quick look at seven organizer boards you can build— from a cardboard-box kiosk to peekaboo exhibit spaces that showcase students' work. 9

Take-Home Notes Make home-school connections with a board that encourages students to communicate school news with their families. 13

Take-Home Activities Inviting activity bags encourage families to reinforce learning at home. 18

Our Classroom Quilt Always appealing, this board is easily adaptable to support any curriculum focus. 22

Window Watch Watch students' observation skills and attention to detail grow all year with this simple dispay. . . 26

Mood Meter How's everyone feeling? Find out with this board! 29

Kindness Cave Watch acts of kindness grow here, along with reading, writing, speaking, and listening skills. 32

Surprise Socks Build science and math skills at a board that will keep students thinking all year. 36

Something to Say Every child gets a chance to speak with a display that introduces conventions of dialogue. 40

Fill-a-Folder Holder Colorful folders showcase students' self-selected work and invite sharing, encouraging an appreciation of one another's strengths. . 43

Portfolio Board: All Aboard This board grows all year, letting students see how they've grown too! 45

The Learning Channel Put a twist on reports and presentations, bringing them to life with this cardboard-box-turned-TV. 48

Tooth Tales This board lets children write about what they know—losing teeth! 51

Daily News Weaving current events (including your classroom's) into the daily routine gives children real-life reasons to read and write. 55

Weather Watch Children have fun dressing cutout kids for the weather—and make science, math, and language arts connections in the process. 58

Fun With a Friend Children team up for ever-changing activities at a board that encourages cooperation. 63

Project Place An inviting assortment of activities guides children in making good use of extra time. 66

Try to Paint Like... Featured artists inspire students' aesthetic development, encouraging confidence in their creative expression. 72

Snapshots Starters for more interactive boards that will keep your students learning all year. 77

From the Authors

Each year, as the start of a new school year rolls around, what bulletin boards do you find yourself planning? How often will you change them during the year? Bulletin boards are an integral part of your classroom environment. They can do more than bring in a new season and brighten a space—good bulletin boards enliven learning and make children feel at home in the classroom. But if you're like most teachers, you find that they don't always come easy. You want your bulletin boards to be neat and creative and to make meaningful learning connections. How can you bring all of this together and still have time for the rest of your job? Put your boards in the hands of your students!

Bulletin boards can become exciting places for students to learn—displays that grow and change as the year progresses, engaging students right from the start. This book is designed to guide you and your students as you create interactive displays that will support your curriculum from September to June. Because these boards will evolve over time, you can plan on putting them up and leaving them up, making small changes to move them forward throughout the year.

For example, start the year with an easy-to-implement classroom quilt that invites children to draw themselves on paper quilt squares and then arrange them to form a quilt. This beginning-of-the-year display helps develop a sense of community in the classroom—an important first step. Over the course of the year, students can change the squares to reflect seasons, holidays, themed units, and so on. Appealing in its simplicity, this display engages students every step of the way—from choosing a topic to designing the quilt squares and planning the finished arrangement. And by the end of the year, students will have completed enough squares to make individual quilts—each square a lovely reminder of the year's activities.

The other interactive displays in this book are equally effective. Each is designed to grow from one month to the next, with the potential to last all year. Not only do these boards relieve you of the time-consuming task of creating new boards with every season or approaching holiday, they add continuity to your program and allow children to revisit concepts and build on what they know.

What's Inside

In the pages that follow, you'll find directions for getting your interactive bulletin boards started, plus lots more.

◎ **Photographs:** To guide you and your students in building these boards, each is accompanied by a photo that shows what one classroom's display looks like. As students interact with the boards, they'll put their own stamp on them.

◎ **Learning Links:** Each board can support your curriculum in numerous ways. This section suggests a few possibilities.

◎ **Border Box:** There's nothing wrong with commercial borders, but this section suggests easy ways to tailor-make eye-catching borders for each board.

◎ **Building the Board:** Most of the materials you'll need are easy to find and inexpensive. (See Help From Home.) Craft paper is often mentioned in the materials list—nonfading paper that comes in rolls makes putting up backgrounds a breeze. From putting down the background paper to adding finishing touches, this section also guides you in getting your boards up.

◎ **Seasonal and Holiday Links:** Suggestions for making special changes throughout the year keep student interest strong.

◎ **Variations:** Bulletin boards can be varied to reflect the needs, interests, or skill levels of your students. The ideas here suggest some of the options available.

◎ **Teaching With the Board:** Here you'll find activities that take each bulletin board further, including literature links, math and science spin-offs, language arts mini-lessons, and more.

◎ **Reproducible Pages:** From templates to journal pages, these reproducibles are ready to use with your students. Keep their interests and needs in mind as you use these pages. Rather than limit children to what is on the reproducibles, use them as a starting place and see what students have to add.

HELP FROM HOME

Part of what makes bulletin boards appealing is the splash of color they add to a classroom. From the background paper that covers the board to the markers students use for various activities, having bright, fresh materials on hand is a plus. To keep your classroom well stocked, consider inviting parents to donate an item or two at the beginning and middle of the year. Craft paper in assorted colors, fadeless construction paper, assorted markers and other writing and coloring tools, straight pins, pushpins, adding machine tape (for borders), plus a bunch of small boxes and other containers (see Handy Holders, page 6) are some of the materials you might request.

Handy Holders

Having tools right where they need them offers children a welcoming invitation to visit the board and take part. Here are a few how-to's for making handy holders.

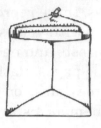

Pin envelopes of all sizes and colors to a board to hold papers, graph markers, and other materials.

Roll the top down on a paper bag. Pin or staple it to the board, or punch a hole and hang it from a pushpin.

Boxes of all shapes and sizes, including milk cartons, make great holders. Punch a couple of holes and hang from straight pins. If you want the contents to show, cut a window out of the box and tape a piece of acetate to the inside.

Hang felt pens in their original boxes. Empty the pens, use pushpins or staples to secure the box from the inside, then restock.

Paper cups of all sizes hold markers, scissors, and other supplies. Staple or punch a hole and hang from a straight pin.

Roll cardboard or sturdy paper and staple one end flat to hold paper and other supplies.

To make see-through pockets to hold numerous pairs of scissors, stitch or staple acetate at regular intervals to a strip of cardboard. You can do the same thing with resealable sandwich bags, stapling several to a strip of cardboard.

Fruit baskets make colorful holders. Use pushpins to attach to your board.

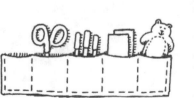

Use tagboard strips to make pockets for holding just about anything.

For a change, tack up clothesline and use clothespins to hang materials such as graph markers or small paperback books. Dangle the clothesline to clip materials vertically.

INTERACTIVE BULLETIN BOARDS • SEPTEMBER TO JUNE
Scholastic Professional Books, 1998

Bright Borders

Materials

- craft paper
- border order form (see page 8)
- folder or clipboard
- pushpins
- markers

Brighten displays by inviting students to help create one-of-a-kind borders. For even more inspiration, start up a classroom Border Company—a bulletin board for creating student-designed borders for your class and others. This "think tank" has great potential as a learning tool (ties in language arts, math, problem-solving, and more) and self-esteem booster. Count on it being one of your students' favorite places to spend time!

Steps

1 Section off an end of a chalkboard or wall. Have children cover it with butcher paper and add a heading that says "The Border Company." Stock a nearby worktable with markers and other materials students might like to use.

2 Together, create a border order form. (See page 8.) Make copies and store in a folder or clipboard near the display.

3 Brainstorm kinds of borders. If possible, take a tour of other classrooms to see a variety of borders. (Bring clipboards to take notes.) List ideas. Let children fill out a border order form for practice, using one of the ideas. Review length of border strips, descriptions, and so on.

4 Guide children in making a few border samples, each about three feet long to show any repeating patterns. Display these with labels at the Border Company board.

5 Have children take border orders for other classrooms and design them. They can also take orders from support staff who have bulletin boards but no students to help with them.

ACCORDION-FOLD BORDERS

You can adapt the pattern shown here to make just about any kind of repeating pattern for your year-round bulletin board borders. Freshen your boards from month to month by changing the border to reflect holiday and seasonal themes. Leaves, pumpkins, evergreen trees, hearts, and flowers are just some of the shapes you can use.

Name _____ Date _____

The Border Company

BORDER ORDER FORM

Name of Client _____

Date _____

Bulletin Board Subject _____

Border Description _____

_____

_____

To Do

Sample Border Only _____

Full Border _____

Border Size

Top _____

Bottom _____

Left Side _____

Right Side _____

Other _____

Total Length of Finished Border _____

Date Needed By _____

Comments _____

_____

_____

Organizers at a Glance

Organization is a big part of a classroom that works. From where you display student work to how you help students get where they need to be on time, there are a few organizational needs that never change. To help you manage those details, here are starters for seven all-year organizer boards—each designed to streamline your day and at the same time build a positive atmosphere in the classroom. For organizer boards that put home-school connections at your fingertips, see Take-Home Notes and Take-Home Activities, pages 13–22.

Class Kiosk

Short on display space? Students will have fun building this one, which, like a kiosk, can provide a space for sharing information and more. Just collect an assortment of boxes. Paint, stack, and use sturdy tape to hold in place. Note that students can place some of the boxes so that they form shelves and other display spaces. Use the display space for notices, student work—whatever you want!

Peekaboo Pictures

These exhibits spotlight children's work in a unique way. Just cover a board with colorful paper, add a sign that says "Peekaboo Pictures," and use pushpins to tack up resealable plastic bags of different sizes. For variety, display some horizontally and others vertically. Cut construction paper to fit inside each bag. Students just drop in their artwork to display!

Birthday Board

If you've got room to display a few fun characters on a wall, you can make this Birthday Board. (For extra appeal, choose characters from favorite stories.) Make a Happy Birthday sign for the birthday child that will stretch across the display. Then have the birthday child climb up on a sturdy stool if need be to join the group (and help hold the sign). Snap a Polaroid to send home. Children love climbing up to become part of a display—and parents and children will enjoy a keepsake.

Pick a Chore... Any Chore

You can set up this display on the back of a door, on part of a larger board, or on an empty wall space. Cover the space with craft paper. Cut out two hands in a card-holding position, and staple them around the sides to create a pocket to hold cards. Write classroom jobs on index cards and slip them into the hand—for example, "bookshelves need straightening." Both you and your students can add jobs anytime you see something that needs to be done. Students who have a few minutes' free time can select jobs to do, then sign the cards when they're finished and deposit them in a special container.

10

Class Contract

Change the content of this Class Contract board to meet any need—for class, the playground, the lunch-room, math time, and so on. Put a friendly face on this board by having children do self-portraits for the border. Arrange them around the edges along with students' names. Write the contract on oaktag and have children sign on a smaller piece underneath.

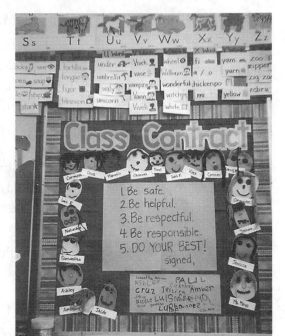

Your Turn to Teach

This display puts your best classroom resource to work—your students. A portable display holds activities that reinforce lessons and skills previously taught. Students select activities and take a turn teaching. You can use this display as a small-group center or to turn those extra minutes in the day (as students are waiting for buses, for lunch, and so on) into productive teaching time. To construct the display, follow these steps:

1. Sew a strip of cloth (about 14 by 60 inches) to a hanger. Fold the cloth over the hanger and stitch in place, or use iron-on tape. (You can also make the display by stapling manila envelopes to a strip of oaktag.)

2. Make pockets of varying sizes—some large enough to hold an 8- by 10-inch piece of paper, some half that size to hold smaller teaching tools such as game cards. Again, you can sew the pockets on or use iron-on tape.

3. Fill pockets with games and activities. A few suggestions follow.

 Place assorted puppets in a pocket, along with simple ideas for using the them.

 Stock a pocket with a set of commercial brainteaser cards.

- Make math fact cards to reinforce math skills.
- Include problem-solving activities. Books by Marilyn Burns, such as *The Book of Think* (Little, Brown, 1976), are good sources.
- Reinforce phonics skills with word games such as Categories. (List categories, such as animals or places, on cards. The "teacher" chooses a category and challenges students to see how many items in that category they can name that start with a certain sound—for example, *dog*, *deer*, *dolphin*, *dodo*, and *dingo* for animals that start with the letter *d*.
- Turn line-up time into learning time. Stock a pocket with activities that will entertain and teach as well as assist children in getting ready to go. Activity suggestions include: line up in alphabetical order by first name/last name; line up by birthdays; line up by height.

Watch the Time

Reinforce time skills, including related vocabulary, with this giant-size watch. Use craft paper (or wrapping paper) and oaktag to construct a wristwatch. Make moveable hands by cutting out minute and hour hands and attaching them to the clock face with a brad. Display the watch on the board with a sign that says "Watch the Time!" Add a timekeeper card (on which you can record the name of the timekeeper for the day) and a container for sentence strips. (The one in this photo is a tray from an easel.) Write (or have students write) special events and times on sentence strips and place them in the holder. Have a timekeeper change the time to show what's coming up next, and post the corresponding sentence strip. To assist children in figuring out the order of events each day, you might also want to post a weekly schedule.

Take-Home Notes

This organizer board will put the many notes you need or want to send home at your fingertips—and your students' too—easing some of the paperwork load that can pile up as well as building students' independence.

BORDER BOX

A simple way to make this board's content stand out is to make a border of take-home notes—just staple one after another all the way around.

LEARNING LINKS

Gaining independence, even in the smallest of ways, is an important part of every young child's experience. As children discover things they can do for themselves, they develop the confidence and self-esteem that lay the foundation for success. This board helps address that goal in small but important ways, putting children in charge of making some of the home-school connections that encourage communication and reinforce learning.

Building the Board

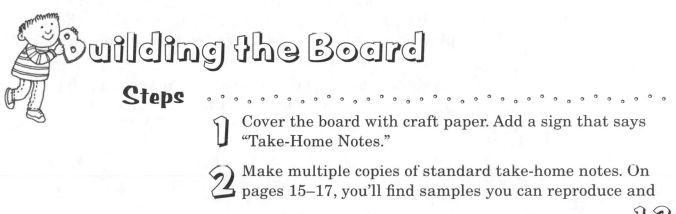

Steps

1 Cover the board with craft paper. Add a sign that says "Take-Home Notes."

2 Make multiple copies of standard take-home notes. On pages 15–17, you'll find samples you can reproduce and

Materials

- craft paper
- take-home notes (see samples pages 15–17)
- straight pins
- envelopes

use. If possible, use different colors for each to help students find the notes they need.

3 Punch two or three holes at the top of each note (left and right sides) and use straight pins to hang on the board. (Be sure the holes are in the same place on each set of notes.)

4 Demonstrate how to slip a note off the straight pins. (If students pull them off carefully, the pins will usually stay put.) Review what the notes are for and let children take turns doing a few trial runs. Ask children to find different notes and give them time to locate them.

5 Have students help themselves to notes as needed. You may need to fill in particulars, though in some cases students may be able to do this themselves.

SEASONAL AND HOLIDAY LINKS

 Though the content of the take-home notes on this board may change little, you can easily change the look—using children's seasonal artwork to decorate the pages. Children can also change the border to reflect seasons and special times of the year.

Variations

Conversation Starters: Spark the kinds of conversations between parents and children that go beyond "What did you do at school today?... I don't remember" with notes that offer prompts about activities and more. In addition to the samples provided on pages 15–17, you might want to include the following notes on your Take-Home Notes board to strengthen home-school connections.

- science investigation note (We explored _____ today. Ask me to tell you about our investigation.)

- generic "ask me to tell you about _____" note (Children can fill in just about anything—a game they played on the playground, new friends they made, a problem, a way they helped someone, and so on.)

- vocabulary-building note (I learned a new word today: _____ . Ask me to tell you what it means.)

Name _____ Date _____

**I had an injury today.
Ask me to tell you what happened.**

____ I rested on a couch.   ____ I used an ice pack.

____ I got a bandage.   ____ It got better by itself.

Name _____ Date _____

**We had an assembly today.
Ask me to tell you about it.**

(Draw a picture about the assembly.)

Name _____ Date _____

**We did a special art project today.
Ask me to tell you about it.**

(Draw a picture about the project.)

Name _____ Date _____

Dear _____,

My homework for tonight is to retell a story we read in class
today. The title of the story we read is _____.
Please set aside 10 minutes to listen to my story and talk
about it with me. I need to bring the bottom portion of this
page back to class by _____.

- -

I told my story to my

____ father   ____ mother

____ sister   ____ brother

____ dog   ____ cat

____ grandparent   ____ babysitter

____ other (_____)

Signed _____
                                    (child)

Name _____ Date _____

**We had a special visitor today.
Ask me to tell you who!**

(Draw a picture about your visitor.)

Name _____ Date _____

I'm running low on supplies. I need to bring:

____ pencils   ____ paper

____ crayons/markers   ____ other (_____)

Name _____ Date _____

**I worked with a buddy today.
Ask me whom I worked with
and what I did.**

(Draw a picture about your work.)

Take-Home Activities

Like Take-Home Notes (see page 13), a Take-Home Activities board will go a long way in building home-school connections—and putting students in charge of helping build these connections.

(see page 13)

BORDER BOX
Brighten the borders of this board with pictures that represent home—for example, pets (dogs, cats, fish, and so on) and a house or other dwelling, decorated in a warm and inviting way.

LEARNING LINKS
You can reinforce any subject with a take-home activity bag. Children will happily share these with parents, paving the way for lots of extra learning and making the home-school connections that research shows are so important to children's success.

Building the Board

Steps

1 Develop a set of take-home activities. Aim for activities that parents and children can fit comfortably into busy afternoons and evenings. (See Variations for suggestions.) Place activities in resealable bags. Add a note to

18

Materials

- take-home activities (see Variations, below, for ideas)
- large resealable bags
- glue
- self-sticking Velcro
- craft paper
- markers
- oaktag
- chart paper

TIP

Store smaller activities, such as sentence strips that children can take home to read with families, in oaktag pockets. To build your supply of activities, invite interested colleagues to set up similar boards. Rotate take-home activities among classrooms to add variety.

parents explaining the bags—what they can keep, what they need to return in the bags, and so on. Glue a strip of Velcro to each bag.

2 Cover a board with craft paper. Add a sign that says "Take-Home Activities."

3 Glue strips of Velcro to the board, spacing them to accommodate the size of the bags. Attach bags to the board.

4 Add a checkout sheet to the board, including name and date checked out/returned.

5 Let children check out activities as they wish. Set up a reserve policy if it becomes difficult for everyone to have a turn.

SEASONAL AND HOLIDAY LINKS

Keep your display fresh all year by featuring a seasonal activity each month. You might decorate a special space for this take-home activity bag—for example, framing it with construction paper and writing "Seasonal Surprise!" at the top. Students will watch it to see what's new. For example, the beginning of the year lends itself to activities about friendship. Or stock a fall surprise bag with harvest activities (a tiny pumpkin in a bag with related activities). January and/or February is a good time to pack surprise bags with materials for exploring African American history. In honor of Groundhog Day, explore shadows in February. For more science connections look at *A Year of Hands-On Science* by Lynne Kepler (Scholastic Professional Books, 1995). This comprehensive resource is organized by months and provides detailed plans and activities for seasonal science links, including reproducible poems, interactive calendars, and pattern pages.

Variations

Sorting Circles: Fill a bag with an assortment of objects (such as buttons, keys, paper clips, pebbles, game pieces, and so on) and a few lengths of string about 36 inches long. Include instructions for forming strings into circles and sorting objects into groups. Offer suggestions for extending the learning: Parents can start the groups and ask children to continue, guessing the rule for each group; children can sort and challenge parents to guess their rule.

The Button Challenge: For a challenging version of Sorting Circles, fill a bag with buttons and sorting strings. How many ways can children and their families find to sort buttons? For example, they might sort by number of holes, color, shape (round/not round), age (these look old/these look new), edges (smooth/not smooth), appearance (fancy/plain), and so on. Include a sheet for recording methods of sorting. How many new ways can families discover?

Bag a Book: Though you can develop literature activity bags based on specific topics students are studying, you can also build them for the sheer enjoyment of a particular book, poem, or both. Try a Tortilla Take-Home Bag. Start with Gary Paulsen's *The Tortilla Factory* (Harcourt Brace, 1998), a lyrical look at how yellow seeds become round tortillas. Add a copy of Gary Soto's poem, "Tortillas Like Africa," from *Canto Familiar* (Harcourt Brace, 1995). And be sure to include a recipe for tortillas so that children and their families can make their own. (See recipe, below; see poem, page 21.) Families can follow up by writing poems about their own tortilla-making experiences, using "Tortillas Like Africa" as a model. Include a family journal in the bag to encourage families to share their poems (and comments) with the class.

Weather Calendar: Package a children's book about weather with a calendar template. Ask families to fill in pictures and words that tell something about the weather each day. Include more weather fun, such as a weather poem, a pinwheel pattern for playing with wind, an unbreakable outdoor thermometer for checking temperature, and so on.

Use with "Tortillas Like Africa," page 21.

MAKE TORTILLAS (adult supervision)

Mix 2 cups masa harina (a kind of cornmeal) with about 1 1/4 cups water and a pinch of salt (if you like). Stir until the water is mixed in and then knead for a few minutes. Divide the dough into 10 to 12 pieces and roll between sheets of waxed paper to make tortillas. What shape are yours? Cook for a few minutes on each side in a lightly greased pan over medium heat. Spread with butter or anything else you like. Eat them warm.

Tortillas Like Africa

When Isaac and me squeezed dough over a mixing bowl,
When we dusted the cutting board with flour,
When we spanked and palmed our balls of dough,
When we said, "Here goes,"
And began rolling out tortillas,
We giggled because ours came out not round, like Mama's,
But in the shapes of faraway lands.

Here was Africa, here was Colombia and Greenland.
Here was Italy, the boot country,
And here was México, our homeland to the south.

Here was Chile, thin as a tie.
Here was France, square as a hat.
Here was Australia, with patches of jumping kangaroos.

We rolled out our tortillas on the board
And laughed when we threw them on the *comal*,
These tortillas that were not round as a pocked moon,
But the twist and stretch of the earth taking shape.

So we made our first batch of tortillas, laughing.
So we wrapped them in a dish towel.
So we buttered and rolled two each
And sat on the front porch—
Butter ran down our arms and our faces shone.

I asked Isaac, "How's yours?"
He cleared his throat and opened his tortilla.
He said, "*¡Bueno!* Greenland tastes like México."

—Gary Soto

From *Canto Familiar* by Gary Soto. Copyright © 1995 by Gary Soto. Used by permission of Harcourt Brace.

Our Classroom Quilt

Here's a board students will delight in setting up during those first few days of school—or anytime.

BORDER BOX

This board calls for nothing more than a quiltlike border that pulls all the quilt squares together. Just run three- to four-inch-wide strips of colorful paper around the outside squares.

TIP

 Pin up a pocket folder and stock each side with different-size squares of paper. Children can use the paper to make mini-quilts of their own.

LEARNING LINKS

You can adapt this board all year to integrate any part of your curriculum. You might start by simply letting children make quilt squares of their faces and write their names. Follow up throughout the year by having children create quilt squares that integrate language arts (squares of rhyming words or favorite storybook characters), math (squares that picture math problems), and science (squares that picture observations or that relate to studies of habitats, dinosaurs, space, and so on).

Building the Board

Steps

1 Cover a display space with craft paper.

2 Create a sign that says "Our Classroom Quilt." Use scraps to form the letters in the style of a crazy quilt.

Materials

◉ craft paper

◉ multicolored nonfading paper squares (about 10 by 10 inches)

◉ fabric and paper scraps

◉ markers, colored pencils, crayons

◉ extra nonfading paper for border

3 Give each child a paper square. To make a quilt of the many faces in your classroom, ask children to illustrate themselves on the squares. (They can color them or use other materials to create collages.)

4 Together, arrange the squares on the floor. When children are satisfied with placement, transfer the quilt squares to the board, leaving a couple of inches between each square.

5 Add a border around the quilt and strips of paper in between the squares (vertically and horizontally).

6 To keep the board fresh, change the quilt squares periodically, using the display to reinforce concepts in your curriculum (see Teaching With the Board, page 24) or to make seasonal connections. As you replace quilt squares with new ones, store those that come down. At the end of the year, children can make individual quilts to take home, using the quilt squares they made during the year.

SEASONAL AND HOLIDAY LINKS

 You'll never be at a loss for ways to keep this board evolving throughout the year. Almost anything you teach will lend itself to quilt-square representations. Some seasonal suggestions follow:

◉ **Fall:** In addition to the pumpkin quilt shown here, leaf rubbings will make a lovely autumn quilt and invite observations of leaf patterns, symmetry, and so on.

◉ **Winter:** Try a night sky quilt. (Winter is a good time for a unit on stars. It gets dark earlier and young children are able to see stars before bedtime.) Let children illustrate what they see on their squares.

◉ **Spring:** Rainy weather is a common spring theme. Explore related vocabulary with a quilt that invites children to write "rainy weather" words on their squares and illustrate them.

Teaching With the Board

Following are just a few of the ways you'll find to use your Classroom Quilt board to integrate your curriculum. Children will have lots of ideas to share too.

History-Makers Quilt: As you look at the contributions of people in any area of study during the year—for example, African Americans in February (African American History Month) or women in March (Women's History Month)—have children feature them on quilt squares. They can create pictures that represent the person and include the person's name, as well as add a few words about their history-makers.

How Big? How big a classroom quilt will 10- by 10-inch squares make? (Children will discover that the answer is in direct proportion to the number of students.) How about if you go with larger (12-inch) or smaller (8-inch) squares? Vary the dimensions and have children estimate and calculate the overall size of the quilt, adding in the size of the border and strips that connect the squares. How many squares will go across and down? These are just a couple of the math connections that will naturally occur as students design new quilts.

Patchwork Patterns: Build geometry skills as students design quilt squares with geometric shapes. (See template, page 25.) Have children color and cut out shapes (you may want to provide multiple copies for each child) and then arrange them on quilt squares. Explore concepts of symmetry and balance as children work. When children are satisfied with their designs, they can glue them in place. Put quilt squares together to make a patchwork quilt.

Synonym Squares: Don't just post a list of synonyms for frequently used words, let children create a quilt of them. For example, use words such as *pretty*, *nice*, and *great* to inspire a synonym quilt. As children's mastery of specific language grows, so will their quilt!

For more teaching ideas, see *Quilting Across the Curriculum*, a thematic, activity-based book by Wendy Buchberg (Scholastic Professional Books, 1996).

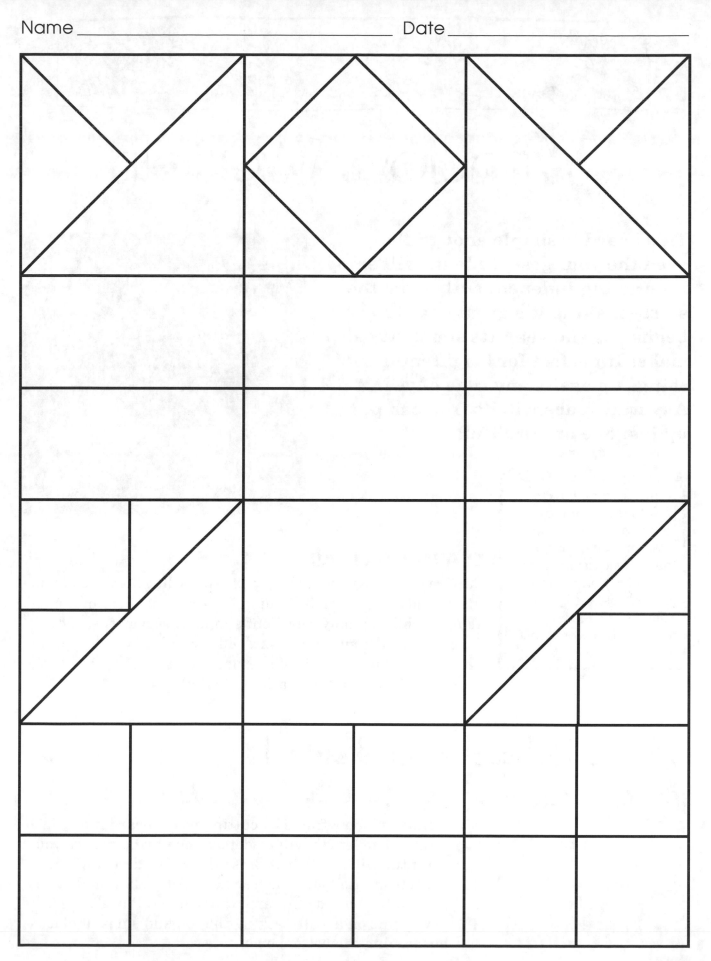

Window Watch

This board is simple enough that even the youngest students will enjoy interacting independently from the start—making it a great board for beginning the year. Its simplicity also makes it perfect for brightening things up easily any time of year. Any wall space will do. You can put up just one or a wallfull.

BORDER BOX

Curtains frame this display to add a homey touch to your classroom. Children can change them to make seasonal or holiday connections—for example, designing curtains with leaf prints for fall or a flowery motif for spring.

LEARNING LINKS

Children of all ages will enjoy picturing what they see outside their windows (and embellishing it with their imaginations!). Younger children may represent simple observations, such as a tree, a bus, the sun in the sky. Older children can be encouraged to show more detail—for example, birds on a branch, the shapes of clouds, and indications of wind.

Building the Board

Steps

1 Build a window frame by cutting posterboard into 2-inch strips. (The length will be determined by how large you want the window to be.) Cross the strips and staple in place to create four or more panes. Add additional strips around the outside to frame the window. Place the window frame on a wall, tacking the top and sides in place but leaving the bottom open.

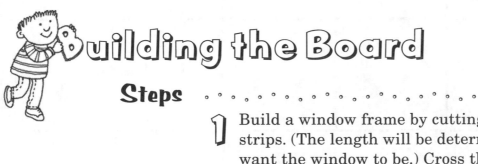

Materials

- brown posterboard
- scissors
- craft paper
- straight pins or pushpins
- assorted art supplies (markers, paints, and so on)
- oaktag (light colored) or drawing paper the size of the window

2 Use craft paper to make curtains for the window. Crease the bottoms to make folds in the curtains. Tack to both sides of the window. Add craft paper tie-backs and a valance if you wish.

3 Have a couple of children team up to make a window scene. Suggest that they take a careful look outside and then include their observations in the picture. (Precut paper to size so that children's pictures will fit securely inside the window frame. Help children slide the picture into the window frame from the bottom, pushing it into place at the top. (The picture should stay in place. If it doesn't, put a couple of pieces of rolled tape on the back and press the picture to the wall.)

4 Let children change the window scene periodically.

SEASONAL AND HOLIDAY LINKS

 Precut sets of curtains (side panels and valence) so that children can redecorate as they like. They can change the curtains to make seasonal and holiday connections—for example, a harvest print for fall, snowflakes in winter, and flowers in spring.

Variations

Play House:

Turn an appliance box into a playhouse complete with windows. Construct windows by cutting openings in the box. Let children design them first, drawing the window shapes on the cardboard for you to cut out. They can draw traditional rectangular-shaped windows, round windows, arched windows, French doors—a look through a home decorating magazine will inspire more. Add muntins (the strips that separate panes) and paint. Have children design window scenes and then tape them in place from the outside. (They'll see the scenes from the inside.)

Window Notes:

To involve all children on a regular basis, keep a class learning log near the window display. Have children who paint the picture record or dictate their observations. Invite other children to add notes as they wish. Remind your window watchers to date their entries. Try to find a few minutes each day to let children share their entries with the whole class, a friend, or a small group.

Teaching With the Board

Use these activities to strengthen the observation skills that students utilized on the Window Watch board.

What's New?

Children can play this simple game just about anywhere. Just gather an assortment of small objects on a tray and let children take a look. (Small groups work best.) Ask children to close their eyes while you add an object. Have them open their eyes and take another look. What's new? As a variation, remove an object instead of adding one. Ask: "What's missing?"

Learning to Look:

In *The Book of Think* (Little, Brown, 1976), Marilyn Burns writes about "mental wall number one: not seeing what's under your very nose." She asks readers, "Without looking, what color socks are you wearing?…When you're getting dressed in the morning, which sock do you put on first?…When you clasp your hands…which thumb is on top?" To help readers realize just how much they haven't bothered to notice, the author offers a few more tests. Try a few with your students to exercise their observation powers. Follow up by inviting students to take a new (and maybe closer) look at each:

⊙ Think of the telephone. Draw a picture of it. Which letters go where?

⊙ Answer true or false: Your bedroom door opens in toward your bedroom.

⊙ Imagine you're in your kitchen. What's usually on the counter?

⊙ Without looking around, write down the names of your classmates who wear glasses.

Before and After:

To further test students' powers of observation, ask them to draw pictures of the school entryway from memory. Have children label these pictures "before." Take children outside with paper and pencil to draw the entryway as it is. Encourage them to really look at this area, noticing small details such as grass growing in the cracks of a sidewalk, the number of doors, building materials around the front door, and so on. Ask children to label these pictures "after." Have them compare their before and after pictures. What did they miss in their first drawings? What new observations are reflected in their second drawings?

Mood Meter

Encourage children's awareness of the many moods we all experience by creating this display together.

LEARNING LINKS

This board invites children to share feelings, developing vocabulary for these feelings in the process. Not only will this strengthen children's communication skills but it can help them recognize that we all have "ups and downs" now and then and learn to deal with these feelings in a positive manner.

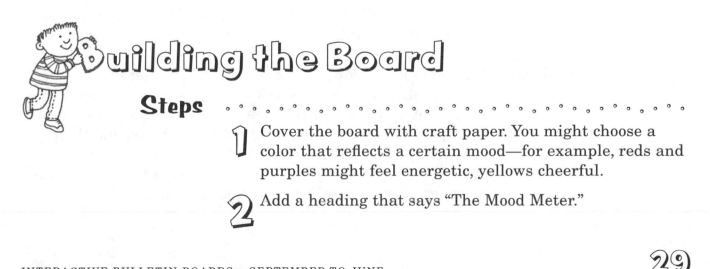

Building the Board

Steps

1 Cover the board with craft paper. You might choose a color that reflects a certain mood—for example, reds and purples might feel energetic, yellows cheerful.

2 Add a heading that says "The Mood Meter."

Materials

- craft paper
- oaktag
- sticky notes

3 Beneath the heading, make and display a "mood meter," placing purple, pink, and yellow (or any other three colors) together as shown. Write the words "working on it," "so-so," and "great" on the mood meter from right to left. Add an arrow in the middle.

4 Post three pieces of oaktag beneath the meter for students to record their moods. You can add pictures of children's faces with hands holding each board if you like.

5 To the right of the oaktag, post a sheet of paper about 12 by 18 inches. Have children write their names on sticky notes and stick them on the paper. When they're ready to post their mood for the day, they just pick up their names and place them in the correct spot on the meter. The further left they go, the better their moods.

SEASONAL AND HOLIDAY LINKS

 Add seasonal cheer to the Mood Meter from month to month with decorations children create. In any given month, talk about seasonal events. Let children suggest something about the season that makes them feel good—for example, apples in September, pumpkins in October, and so on. Children might like to sign up in teams to take over decorating the board each month in this manner.

Variations

Mood Sliders: Children can make individual mood meters with sentence strips, writing the words "working on it," "so-so," and "great" at the beginning, middle, and end of the strip (maybe even shading in the strip with graduating color). Have them each write their name on the strip and use a paper clip to attach an arrow cut from tagboard. To show how they're feeling, have children just slide the arrow to whatever part of the strip best matches their mood.

Feeling Families: Instead of just having children place their names under the meter to show their moods, ask them to write words on sticky notes that describe how they feel. They can also explain their feelings if they like. To encourage children to expand their vocabulary of words that describe feelings, set up charts to record "feeling families"—for example, words to more specifically describe sadness, happiness, and so on.

Teaching With the Board

You know how much moods can affect the classroom atmosphere. Use these ideas to turn them into teaching tools:

Bad Mood Buster:

Share *Spinky Sulks* by William Steig (Farrar, Straus & Giroux, 1988), the story of a boy who goes into a solid sulk over, well, not much of anything. Follow up by discussing moods children find themselves in. Can anyone relate to Spinky and his inability to stop sulking? Ask: "Why do you think nothing anyone did seemed to get Spinky to stop sulking? If you were Spinky's friend, what would you have done?"

I Feel Better:

Brainstorm ways to change a bad mood, asking: "What kinds of things do you do to get out of a bad mood?" Offer suggestions, such as taking a few minutes for some time alone, playing a favorite song, and "venting" to a friend. Try to accomodate some of the ideas, for example, providing a space students can go to have their own time outs, making time for students to share feelings with one another, and keeping some cassettes handy (headphones, too, so that individual students can plug in for a lift).

Kindness Cave

Transform brown paper into a cave that children will watch with rapt attention for signs of kind acts being committed. (Pooh and Piglet—or any stuffed animals—"come out" when you or a student observes a kind act. You or the child who observes the act write about it on a flower or stone outside the cave for all to see.)

BORDER BOX

Personalize a border by having children write their names on sentence strips. Tack them up around the edges to create a border, thus making every child a part of the Kindness Cave from the start.

LEARNING LINK

Kindness is one of those life lessons that needs to be woven into classroom activities every day. This board enables you to integrate that lesson with other classroom learning goals. As children develop this board over time, they will also have daily opportunities to speak, listen, write, and read—the cornerstones of any language arts curriculum. As the board builds every day, so will students' positive feelings about their good deeds.

Building the Board

Steps

1 Make the inside of the cave by stapling black paper in the center as shown in the photo on page 32.

2 Create a cave by bunching a large piece of brown paper around the black paper to create a semicircle or dome. Leave space between the inside of the brown paper and the black paper. Staple in place along the outside edge only. Cut away the center of the brown paper to reveal the inside (black) of the cave.

Materials

⊙ black and brown craft paper

⊙ stapler

⊙ Velcro

⊙ glue

⊙ construction paper (assorted colors)

⊙ scissors

3 Place pictures of Pooh and Piglet (or use two stuffed animals or pictures of any other friendly characters) inside the cave. (If the brown paper is bunched a little, you can slide them in.) Glue Velcro to the inside of each side of the cave as well as to the backs of the characters. Glue two more pieces of Velcro to either side of the cave opening. This will allow you to easily place the characters inside the cave or bring them out.

4 Above the cave, add a sign that says "Kindness Cave." Above the cave opening, add a sign that says "Pooh and Piglet (substitute other names if using other characters) are peeking out...to see what kindness is all about."

5 Let children cut out flowers and large stones from paper and add to the board around the cave.

6 Demonstrate how the board works by observing an act of kindness. Bring Piglet and Pooh out of the cave and have them "whisper" to you about what they saw. Write about the act of kindness on a stone, mentioning the child's name.

7 Children can follow up by letting you know when they spot acts of kindness in the classroom. Have them bring Piglet and Pooh out of the cave to "tell" what happened and then write about (or dictate) it on stones or flowers. Keep plenty of paper nearby for making fresh flowers and new stones so that children can easily add to the display.

SEASONAL AND HOLIDAY LINKS

Let children change the display to reflect the seasons—for example, replacing the flowers and rocks with leaves and pumpkins for fall, snowflakes and snowpeople for winter, baby animals or budding trees for spring, and so on. Integrate other areas of study, such as a unit on apples, harvest, or trees, by "planting" a tree and changing it each month to show its life cycle.

Variations

Good-Deed Doers:

For older children, create a simple three-column chart to record names, deeds, and feelings, as shown. Label the chart "Kindnesses We Have Known" (or whatever your students suggest). Add a box of markers (pin the box to the board for easy access), and students will be all set to recognize good-deed doers in the classroom.

Tell Us What You Think:

Another wonderful way to encourage a caring atmosphere in the classroom is by setting up a "Special Person" display that spotlights a different child each week. As shown, all you have to do is cover a board, add a sign ("Special Person") and a sentence strip that says "Tell us what you think about _____." Write each child's name on a sentence strip and trim to fit the blank. Punch a hole in one end of each name strip and hang on the board with a straight pin. If possible, have a Polaroid camera handy to photograph the featured child each week. (Or ask parents to send in photos at the beginning of the year.) Post the picture(s) and chart paper or posterboard, add a box of markers and pushpins, and let students pay tribute to the special person of the week! They can write what they like about the person on the paper, tack up pictures and other comments, and so on. You'll find that this board does more than boost children's self-esteem. It will help them discover the pleasure in giving genuine compliments as they notice and appreciate the good in others and brighten someone's day by expressing those things.

34

Teaching With the Board

Kindness goes hand in hand with caring. And an atmosphere of caring is vital to building success in the classroom. In *Creating a Caring Classroom* (Scholastic Professional Books, 1997), Nancy Letts describes successful classrooms she had visited. "I couldn't quite name what I was seeing, but I was sure it was there. Then I noticed that in some rooms, children went out of their way to help other kids. In those same classrooms children cooperated, rather than fiercely competing." The following suggestions from *Creating a Caring Classroom* show how you can build on the successes in your classroom by making caring an integral part of education:

Listen In: Audiotape a class meeting one day. Together, listen for signs of caring in the classroom. Listen for words that convey caring. (For example, what do you or students say when someone is talking too long?) Listen for thoughtful dialogue—you or your students offering suggestions in a caring way to a classmate who has a problem. Listen for evidence that you and your students give one another time to formulate responses. Together, set a "kindness and caring" goal for the next meeting or for the class in general.

Parent Support: Planning a new unit? Give a few parents a call. Ask if there's anything special they'd like to see included. For example, Letts describes a teacher planning a unit on women's history. She called students' mothers, explaining the unit and asking "Are there women who you think should be included in our study?" Inviting parents to contribute in this way enriches the curriculum and sends a powerful message about caring to parents and children.

Build Caring Communities: Extend kindness beyond the walls of the classroom to include members of the community. Identify a need and plan a service project—for example visiting seniors, reading to preschool children, or beautifying a corner of the playground.

Surprise Socks

Turn odd socks into a year of science and math skill-building with this board. It's easy! Children hang socks from a yarn clothesline, placing objects inside. What attributes can children identify to help them make educated guesses about what's inside each sock?

BORDER BOX

A border of colorful pictures of socks is simple and appealing. Children can take turns coloring them on strips of paper, or they can color and cut out socks and then glue them around the edges of the board.

LEARNING LINKS

When children sort objects into groups, they're analyzing attributes—ways the objects are alike or different. Surprise Socks builds on these classifying and categorizing skills to develop logical reasoning. Using the same skills required to sort objects into groups, students analyze attributes—this time without actually seeing the objects. They can then apply the information they gather to draw reasonable conclusions— a skill with many everyday applications.

Building the Board

Steps

1 Cover a bulletin board with bright paper. Have children color a border of socks on strips of white paper. Add a sign ("Surprise Socks") and a sentence strip that says "Describe the object." Post a chart with two sections labeled "Description" and "Guesses."

Materials

- craft paper
- crayons or markers
- white paper, cut into strips for border design
- posterboard or chart paper
- stapler
- yarn
- clothespins
- odd socks
- individual response sheets (see page 39)

2 Use a stapler to attach yarn to the board from one side to the other. (You'll probably need to run the yarn across the board several times to accommodate all students.)

3 Clip on clothespins and odd socks. (Ask each child to bring one from home. Bring in a few extras for children who do not have a sock.)

4 One at a time, let students place a surprise in their socks. (You can rotate every day or two or each week.) Have children feel the socks to find out which one holds the surprise and then, without looking inside, feel the object and record descriptive words and guesses on the chart.

5 At the end of a specified period of time, let the student reveal what's inside the sock. Guide a discussion to help children analyze their guesses.

- Which descriptive words were most helpful in making educated guesses?

- Which guesses are most logical? Least? (For example, if a golf ball is hidden inside, children might say the object is round. Though both oranges and golf balls fit that description, noticing that the object is hard would help children eliminate orange from the possibilities.)

- After students have had a chance to see the object, ask, "What other words describe the object?"

SEASONAL AND HOLIDAY LINKS

 To celebrate special times throughout the year, set aside days or weeks to feature seasonal sock surprises. Ask children to choose objects that represent a season, holiday, or other special time of the year. For example, spring socks might hold baseballs, bulbs, seeds, even a handful of soil. Children can also coordinate sock colors with seasons and special days.

Variations

° °

Attribute Elimination: Have children each place an object in their socks. Tack a number up next to each sock for identification purposes. Then play Attribute Elimination, a game of logical reasoning. Choose an object from one of the socks, and list attributes of this object on the board. (Do this when students are out of the room.) When children return, have them try to guess which sock holds the object described and guess what it is. Post paper for recording names and guesses (sock number and object).

A Surprise in Each Sock: Make individual charts for each child to post near his or her sock. (See page 39.) Let each child put something in his or her sock. Children can analyze one another's socks, recording descriptive words and guesses. At the end of the week, let each child reveal his or her sock surprise. Again, guide a discussion to analyze attributes and logical guesses.

Themed Surprises: Identify one attribute all surprises must have in common, such as "round." Have each child bring in an object that fits this criterion, place it in his or her sock, and tack up a description/guesses record sheet. Let children identify attributes of one another's sock surprises and record guesses. At the end of a specified period of time, have children reveal their objects. What attributes helped them differentiate one object from another?

Teaching With the Board

The suggestions that follow will help you use Surprise Socks to encourage students' attention to detail.

Home-School Connection: Send a note home explaining how to set up a sock surprise game at home. You might also want to send home multiple copies of the Surprise Socks chart. Family members can take turns challenging one another with surprises in a sock. Invite children to share some of the surprises and their guesses.

Assessment and Evaluation: As children analyze more and more sock surprises and participate in follow-up discussion to evaluate clues and guesses, you should notice that their descriptive words have become more specific and their guesses more logical (which may not always mean correct). List the words children use to describe the same object. Notice the detail in their descriptions.

One and Only: Take a bag of walnuts. They all look the same, right? When your students get done with this activity, they won't. In *The Book of Think*, Marilyn Burns describes The Walnut Game, guaranteed to boost your students' observation skills and their ability to notice details (useful in analyzing attributes on the Surprise Socks board). Start by giving each child a walnut. Have children study their walnuts, exploring them until they're sure they could pick their walnuts out of a group. Put the nuts back in the bag, mix them up, then spread them out. Can children identify their walnuts? What details make their walnuts unlike any other?

Surprise Socks

Describing Words	Guesses

My Sock Surprise is _____.

(Don't fill this in until everyone has made a guess.)

Something to Say

This simple board channels all that energy students have for talking and teaches them how to transform it into writing.

BORDER BOX

Each time students make new speech bubbles for this board, glue those that have been removed to strips of paper and tack them around the edges.

LEARNING LINKS

In a class discussion there's often not time to hear from every child. This board lets every child respond thoughtfully to a question you or a classmate asks. It also segues nicely into mini-lessons on conventions of dialogue such as use of quotation marks and speaker tags. (See Teaching With the Board, page 42.)

40

Building the Board

Steps

1. Let students draw and frame pictures of their faces. Ask children to make name tags to display with their framed faces.

2. Provide templates for speech bubbles. Have children each cut out several to add to a class supply. (Fill a box pinned to the board with speech bubbles so they're always available.)

3. Display faces anywhere—a long stretch of wall inside or outside the classroom works well. Add name tags beneath or next to faces. Let children "speak," responding on speech bubbles to questions you ask and placing them next to their faces.

4. With each new question you ask, have students add new speech bubbles. They can tack up the old speech bubbles around the edges to create a border for the board.

Materials

- construction paper (or other art paper)
- colored pencils, markers, crayons
- white paper

SEASONAL AND HOLIDAY LINKS

 Use this display at times to have children respond to questions related to seasonal and holiday topics. For example, as changes in seasons approach, ask questions like "What are some ways you know winter/spring/summer is on the way?" or "What do you like most about winter/spring/summer?" Connect with special holidays too.

Variations

Weekend News: Let children use the board on Mondays to share news of their weekends. Get them started by asking: "What would you tell a friend about your weekend?" Give children time to read the display to catch up on the news.

Face Changers: Let children decorate the pictures of their faces on the board for different seasons or holidays. They might add masks for Halloween, caps for baseball season, and so on.

Teaching With the Board

From author studies to at-home assignments, here are a few ideas for using speech bubbles as teaching tools.

Speak Your Mind: Use this board to invite every child to "speak up" in response to questions or discussion topics. For example, if you've just completed a Tomie dePaola author study, after spending some time discussing the various stories, you might ask: "Who was your favorite character? Why?" Rather than have children share aloud (which sometimes means that children who need more "think time" or feel uneasy contributing to large group discussions are left out), let them take time to record thoughts in speech bubbles. Children will enjoy "hearing" what their classmates have to say as they read the display.

Homework Helper: Have children take home speech bubbles and use them to answer homework questions. For example, children can use the speech bubbles to explain their reasoning for a math problem or record an observation about the weather (or anything else), then add them to the display to show their work.

Quotation Marks and Other Conventions: Speech bubbles are just one way to represent what someone is saying. Introduce conventions of dialogue by rewriting a child's comment on chart paper and asking: "Who said this?" Demonstrate how to use quotation marks and a speaker tag to show what was said and by whom. Write other comments on the chart paper and let children take turns adding quotation marks and speaker tags. Reinforce this from time to time by repeating the activity with new speech bubbles.

Fill-a-Folder Holder

Colorful folders on a bulletin board or other wall space showcase student shares—stories, artwork, favorite authors, current events, and so on.

BORDER BOX

Children can draw pictures of themselves and friends, cut them out, and place them head to toe and arm to arm around the board. For a twist, have them do their drawings in black and white, like the border shown here.

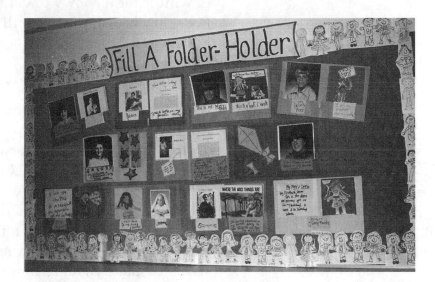

LEARNING LINKS

How many times have you heard, "This is special to me because…" There never seems to be enough time for sharing in a classroom, though it's something every child seems to love. This board gives each child an opportunity to share and sends the message that all children have something valuable to contribute. The positive feelings this board generates will spill over into the day as children develop pride and confidence in their learning and themselves.

Building the Board

Steps

1 Cover the board with craft paper. Add a sign that says "Fill-a-Folder Holder" and a border. Arrange open folders on the board and staple in place.

2 Enlarge photos of children (photocopies are fine). Children can select folders to use and place their photos (or self-portraits) and something they'd like to share in either side. Children can change their shares as often as they like. (Or you can give directions to support a teaching focus.)

3 Let children browse the board, removing contents they want to look at and replacing them when they're finished.

SEASONAL AND HOLIDAY LINKS

Simply change the color of the folders at this board for seasonal appeal. Start with fall colors in September, orange and black for October, and white in winter for a snowy effect. Pinks and reds will warm up a February board, pastels will bring Spring into the room in March and April.

Variations ∘

Display Options: If your classroom doesn't have enough display space to fit a folder for every child at the same time, rotate groups of children. Children will look forward to their display time and to seeing the work of each new group. To reuse folders for each group, have students write their names on paper, decorate, then paper clip the tags to the inside pockets. When it's time for another group to take a turn, students can just unclip and replace the old tags with their own. Or use bulletin board strips to make room to hang everyone's folders.

Teaching With the Board

You can use the folders as informal portfolios for students' work. Following are ideas for organizing their contributions.

Theme Folders: Suggest themes each month for filling folders. For example, in September students might write or draw pictures about new friends, first days of school, and so on. Other prompts you can use include "My Collection," "A Trip I Took," any theme unit you're working on, "Best Friends," "An Important Event in My Life," and "New Rules I'd Make for School." Let children suggest topics too.

Show-and-Tell: Many teachers bring children together for "sharing" at some point in the day—a time when children can tell about something special that's happened, share a favorite toy, and so on. Use the board to let "share" go on a little longer. Children can use their folders to display postcards from faraway friends and family members, to share written stories about events outside of school, even to share small objects (pinned up in sandwich bags).

Portfolio Board: All Aboard

Students will watch this board grow all year as they proudly add pictures and stories to their individual bulletin board books—creating portfolios that reflect growth over time as well as keepsakes that they and their families will treasure.

BORDER BOX

In keeping with the train concept of this board, have children make one long train that goes all the way around the border. You might provide templates for different kinds of cars or books students can use as reference. Have children use the same size paper so that the individual pieces will more easily make a border.

LEARNING LINKS

Portfolios allow you, your students, and parents to see growth as the year progresses. Rather than routing around for scattered samples, a portfolio puts an organized sampling of students' work in one easy-to-access place. This bulletin board lets students build informal portfolios, showcasing their best work with new samples each month. As students watch their stacks grow, you can look for development in writing, concepts, artwork, and so on. Use the pages at conference time too.

Building the Board

Steps

Materials

- brown craft paper
- white craft paper
- paint, paintbrushes
- construction paper
- markers, crayons
- scissors

1 Cover the board with brown craft paper. Attach strips of white paper, weaving them across the board. Have students use black paint or marker to make train tracks on the white strips.

2 Add a sign that says "All Aboard for _____." Fill in the name of the month (changing it each month as students add new samples).

3 Have students create individual "train cars" to frame their work. They can attach wheels to a piece of construction paper, write their names on the cars, and place them one after another on the track. Make sure students' names are visible on each car.

4 Landscape the display according to the season. As the year progresses, students can change the scenery—for example, adding falling leaves and pumpkins in the fall and snowflakes in winter.

5 Decide on a topic for the first piece. For example, in September you might ask students to picture themselves on the first day of school. Each month post a new topic, making connections with a unit of study, the season, an event, and so on. (See Seasonal and Holiday Links.)

SEASONAL AND HOLIDAY LINKS

 By its nature, this display will change all year as children add new portfolio pieces on a regular basis. You can keep it fresh with seasonal and holiday connections too. Look for calendar connections to guide contributions to the board. From butterfly migration in September to plans for the summer in June, you'll find plenty of ideas students can use as springboards for writing (or drawing).

Variations

Our School:
Create a large image of a school on the board for children to build their month-by-month books. They can landscape the school according to what they see outside their own.

Home to School:
Have students use construction paper strips to create simple houses to frame their work. Display on a board and connect each row with a winding road. Students can add buses and cars, signs, and so on to complete the board.

Teaching With the Board

The informal portfolios developed on this board put pictures of students' progress at your fingertips. Students can use them to set new goals for themselves—and to see how far they've come. You can use them to observe growth from month to month and to tailor individual instruction. Here are a couple of ways you can guide students' month-to-month work to reflect growth in language arts and science:

Book Board: Use the board as a place for students to post responses to poems, stories, and other class reading material. Notice how children's responses change over time. Do they show increased use of specific language? Do students use some of the same techniques they're learning in their writing mini-lessons? What evidence is there of growth in spelling? In sentence development? In content?

Learning Log: Use the board as a class learning log, letting each student add a page each month to record responses to science investigations. Watch for evidence of growth in process skills. How do students communicate observations and ideas? Do observations as recorded (pictures and words) reflect increased use of detail as the months progress? Are children's predictions increasingly based on what they know? Do responses reflect an understanding of key concepts?

The Learning Channel

Here's a board that will have your students begging to research and write reports. It's a cardboard-box-turned-TV, complete with a program guide and backdrops—all created by students. Children can climb in—then tune in to learn!

BORDER BOX

The photo pictured doesn't show a border—a child inside the TV is all you need to pull this display together!

CURRICULUM LINKS

This flexible board will effectively and energetically integrate every subject with reading, writing, speaking, and listening. Students can produce live presentations on any area of study as well as create educational programs that air regularly (perhaps modeled after favorite TV shows).

 Building the Board

Steps

1 Cut out the bottom of the cardboard box. Cut out one side, leaving a border of a few inches around the opening.

2 Position the box on the board (or wall) so that the side opening faces out and the bottom down. Use sturdy tape to attach the box to the board or wall from the inside. Invite children to decorate the box to make a TV.

48

Materials

⊙ large cardboard box (from TV or other large appliance)

⊙ utility knife (for teacher use only)

⊙ sturdy tape

⊙ markers, paint, paintbrushes

⊙ posterboard

⊙ box (about 8 to 10 inches high, 12 inches across)

⊙ chart paper

3 To one side of the box post a TV show sign-up sheet. (Have children record name and show.) To the other side, post a viewer's guide, on which students can list the line-up, and a box to hold backdrops. (Students can make a variety of backdrops to use as they wish.)

4 Brainstorm shows students might produce—related to hobbies, projects, current events, school news, and so on. Children can produce shows independently, with a partner, or in a small group. Suggestions for show time follow:

⊙ Set up regular time slots for children to fill. Depending on your students, you might offer several options ranging from 10 to 20 minutes each.

⊙ Include several sign-up lines for each time slot. Children who only need a few minutes can sign up on one line. Children who need more time can reserve the whole slot.

⊙ Help students learn to turn up the volume when they're on. Have them practice projecting. Can children across the room hear them easily?

SEASONAL AND HOLIDAY LINKS

Plan special shows children can produce throughout the year to make seasonal and holiday connections. For example, September is a good time for a show on bicycle safety, followed by Halloween safety in October. How about a cooking show in November, featuring favorite harvest recipes? Plan a December show featuring Eve Bunting (born in December) and her books. For January (Martin Luther King Day), look at ways racial harmony is promoted in your school and how it can be improved. Plan a show on Groundhog Day and other folklore for February. Your students will come up with lots more ideas. Post a production schedule for these shows, and allow children to sign up to write, direct, and produce them.

Variations

○ ˙ ˙ ○ ˙ ○ ˙ ○ ˙ ○ ˙ ○ ○ ˙ ○ ˙ ○ ˙ ○ ˙ ˙ ○ ○ ˙ ˙ ○ ˙ ○ ˙ ○ ˙ ˙ ○ ○ ˙ ˙ ○ ˙ ○ ○ ˙ ˙ ○ ˙ ○ ˙ ˙ ○ ˙ ○ ○ ˙ ○

This Week in the News: Children can model evening news programs, producing series that take an in-depth look at various topics such as consumer news, health issues, and literacy. For example, they might produce a four-part series on nutrition and fitness for children, looking at healthy ways to start the day, preparing nutritious bag lunches, exposing the fat content in fast-food meals, and interviewing the physical education teacher about the benefits of exercise. These types of shows will strengthen students'

research and organization skills as they uncover newsworthy information from a variety of sources and decide how to introduce, develop, and conclude the series.

Public Service Announcements: Your students are probably familiar with PSAs—those brief radio and TV spots that share messages about safety, health, education, environmental awareness, and so on. Have children work in groups to produce PSAs that focus on relevant topics in their lives. For example, they might produce a PSA about literacy, sharing reasons they're happy they can read, or fitness, encouraging kids and parents to exercise together. After choosing a topic, each group can write up a production plan that includes the rationale, message, and content. Students might like to add catchy tunes and snappy graphics like PSAs they see on TV. When children are ready, let them air their PSAs on the Learning Channel!

Teaching With the Board

You won't have to do much to keep the learning going strong at the classroom Learning Channel. Students will be so eager to produce "shows" about various projects they're working on that you'll probably have the Learning Channel booked for weeks at a time. To make the most of students' TV time, here are a few things you can do:

Every Student Stars: Not every child feels completely comfortable getting up in front of groups to speak, but there are many ways for everyone to be part of a production. From scripting a show to creating backdrops and planning commercials, there's something to showcase each child's strengths. Children who have programs they want to create but not present can audition others to play the parts—reporters, actors, or whatever the show calls for.

Beginnings, Middles, Endings: Guide children in preparing their shows by analyzing shows they like to watch.

◉ What kinds of beginnings make viewers want to keep watching?

◉ How do the middles of shows students watch keep them tuned in?

◉ What makes an ending satisfying? (Look at cliff-hangers, surprise endings, and so on.)

Tooth Tales

Losing teeth is a big part of the early grades. Children wiggle their teeth, waiting for the day one feels loose. They await the tooth fairy when those teeth come out and eagerly share stories about what happened. This board builds on this natural part of childhood, giving children's tooth tales the special attention they deserve.

BORDER BOX

Smiling teeth decorate the borders of the board pictured here. Make one as a model, then let children make their own. (They can use the template on page 54 as a pattern.) Encourage children to be creative. They might decorate their teeth by adding faces, hair, and so on. Put teeth together around the edges of the board.

LEARNING LINKS

Reading and writing come together in this display as children write or dictate stories to share with classmates. They'll enjoy comparing stories about a common experience.

Building the Board

Steps

1 Cover a board with bright paper. Add a sign that says "Tooth Tales."

2 Pin both boxes to the board. Label one "Blank Teeth," and stock it with copies of page 54. Label the other "Tooth Tales."

Materials

- craft paper, assorted colors
- pushpins
- markers
- 2 small boxes (one to hold teeth story templates, one to hold completed stories)
- tooth template (see page 54)
- chart paper

3 Draw a smiling face on a large sheet of craft paper. Pin it to the board.

4 Let children who have lost teeth tell their stories, writing them on copies of the reproducible and placing them in the "Tooth Tales" box. Add to the display with related graphs. (See Teaching With the Board, page 53.)

TIP

 Make "hairpieces" and additional faces and accessories so that children can change the face on the board. Pin them up next to the board, or store them on the board

in a large envelope. You and your students can add to this "quick change" display throughout the year to give the display face a new look now and then.

SEASONAL AND HOLIDAY LINKS

Add tooth toppers to celebrate seasons and holidays—for example, masks for Halloween, rain hats, earmuffs, baseball caps, birthday crowns, and so on.

Variations

° °

Tooth Tales Big Book: Have students write and display their tooth tales on chart paper. Add each page to a class big book of tooth tales, binding pages with O-rings. (You can easily open these up to insert new pages.) When you introduce the board, have students make a front and back cover for the book. Laminate covers and inside pages (after completion) for durability.

Tooth Tags: Add medallions to the board that read "I lost a tooth! Ask me to tell you about it." Let children pin these to their clothes to wear when they lose a tooth.

Teaching With the Board

Investigate teeth with activities that integrate science and math.

The Way Teeth Work: Explore the function of teeth with this simple activity. Provide slices of apples, carrots, and other crunchy foods. Have children take a bite, noting the teeth they use to bite. Have children chew, noting the teeth they use to chew. Ask: "How do we use our front teeth? How do we use our back teeth? What do you notice about the front teeth that makes them good biting teeth?" (They're sharp.) "What do you notice about the back teeth that makes them good chewing teeth?" (Molars have a bigger surface than front teeth, making them good for grinding food—an important first part of the digestive process.)

How Many? Provide small mirrors and let children open up and count. How many on the top? On the bottom? Have children record top, bottom, and total. Graph results. What is the range of students' totals? What are some possible explanations?

Graphing Teeth: Add related graphs to your board. A few ideas follow.

⊙ Graph how many children still have all their teeth, how many have lost one, and how many have lost more than one. Let children use sticky notes to create the graph. Leave the graph up, letting children move their markers from the "still have all my teeth" side to one of the other columns when they lose teeth.

⊙ Graph favorite flavors/kinds of toothpaste.

⊙ Graph "Do you like going to the dentist or not?" (Believe it or not, some children will say they like to go—not just for the toothbrushes and other goodies they get at the end but for the movies they get to watch with the video glasses in some dentists' offices.)

Tooth Tales

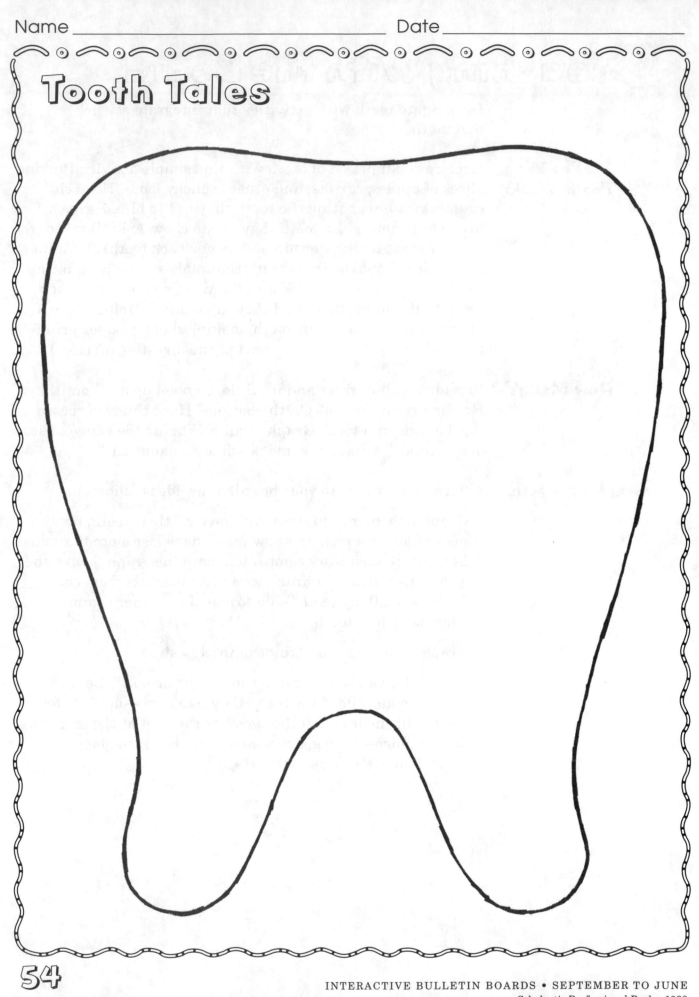

Daily News

This board weaves current events into the classroom routine, at the same time giving children real-life reasons to read and write. It will also go a long way in boosting self-confidence as children take turns being "reporters" and recording the news (class, local, national) for all to read.

BORDER BOX
Cut newspaper into strips for a quick and easy border.

LEARNING LINKS
From looking at letters to recognizing writing devices in head-lines and leads, children will find that newspapers are full of classroom connections. You can integrate those connections by looking at daily newspapers and by having students report the news in their own lives. This board has other benefits as well. As daily news becomes part of the classroom routine, children will grow into informed citizens—knowledgeable and interested in what's happening in the world around them.

Building the Board

Steps

1 Cover a bulletin board with craft paper and use strips of newspaper to make a border. Cut out letters from the newspaper to create a heading that says "Daily News."

Materials

⊙ craft paper
⊙ newspaper
⊙ scissors
⊙ posterboard (9 pieces)
⊙ stapler
⊙ chart paper

2 Attach posterboard, labeling one piece "Headline News" and the others with the days of the week. (You can do weekdays only or include weekends.)

3 Add a stack of chart paper to each. Divide the Headline News chart paper into two sections labeled "Local" and "National." Include space for datelines (identify date and origin of story) and bylines (reporter's name) on each.

4 Roll the last piece of posterboard into a cylinder and staple it to the bottom right corner of the board. Use this to "deliver" the newspaper each morning.

5 Schedule student reporters for the week. Have the day's reporter use the newspaper to find a local and national news story and record a sentence or two about them on the board. (You can let the child choose the story or have a class discussion about the news, then let the reporter choose from among those stories.) Follow up by discussing class news as the reporter records it. (Emergent writers may prefer to dictate.)

6 As students become familiar with the process, they can set up their own chart paper for the days they are reporters. You can save each day's news, binding it each week for students to reread, or let reporters take home their news stories at the end of each day.

SEASONAL AND HOLIDAY LINKS

 Take seasonal and holiday headlines from local papers and post them on the board, letting student reporters tell the stories themselves. These headlines might have seasonal (Snowstorm Closes Schools) or holiday (Martin Luther King, Jr., Remembered) connections. Be sure to provide children with resources if necessary.

Variations

Team Reporters: Rather than schedule one child per day to report on both class and outside news, have children work in teams to share the job—one reporting on local and national news, the other on class news.

More Than the News: Newspapers hold more than the daily news—they've got comics, advertisements, even advice columns! Enrich your Daily News board by introducing a different component each week. One week, for example, have children write letters to an advice columnist. Guide a couple of students in writing responses. Another week, feature favorite comic strips (both those students find in newspapers and ones they write).

For Emergent Writers:

For young children, put the week's news on one sheet of chart paper. Create three columns: one for names, one for the news, and another for weather reports. Schedule reporters for the week, writing their names on the chart. Have them write a sentence about some class news and then add a picture or a few words to report on the weather.

Teaching With the Board

Explore how different parts of a story help tell the news.

Highlight on Headlines: Focus on headlines one day, noticing techniques writers use to grab your attention. In many cases, alliteration is the answer. Words in a headline that start with the same consonant sound create a rhythm as you read them, making these headlines stand out. "School Has Success Down to a Science" (*New York Times*; January 24, 1998) is one example. Set aside space on the board to post alliterative headlines. Let children use the device in their own writing, creating alliterative headlines for Daily News stories as well as stories they write on their own.

Pictures Tell Stories: Articles aren't the only part of a newspaper that tell the news. Photos do too—as do the cutlines (captions) underneath them. Cut out pictures from a newspaper. Display the photos and file the cutlines. Let children write cutlines to go with the photos, placing them underneath. (More than one student can write a caption for each photo—lining them up under the photos they go with.) Eventually, post the actual cutline and discuss different ways of looking at the same thing.

For More Information: The Newspaper Association of America, in conjunction with the International Reading Association and the National Council for the Social Studies, offers materials for teaching with newspapers. Write to IRA Headquarters, 800 Barksdale Rd., P.O. Box 8139, Newark, Delaware 19714-8139, or call (302) 731-1600.

Weather Watch

Great for young children, this board combines math, language arts, science, and personal skills with hands-on weather explorations.

LEARNING LINKS

Whether they're deciding what to wear in the morning or going outside to play, children experience the weather in their world every day. That's what makes weather a natural year-round curriculum connector. Weather is full of meaningful language experiences—we talk about the weather, listen to and read weather reports to decide what to wear and do, write about it in letters to grandparents and faraway friends. Temperature and precipitation can be measured, weather conditions can be graphed and used to make predictions, and more—all examples of ways we use math and science in our daily lives.

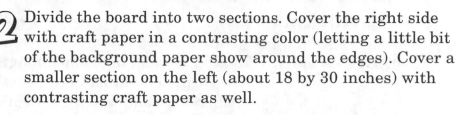

uilding the Board

Steps

Materials

- craft paper, assorted colors
- Weather Graph (see page 62)
- pocket notebook
- straight pins
- scissors
- pushpins
- markers
- chart paper

1 Cover a bulletin board with craft paper. Add a border (see Border Box) and a sign that says "Weather Watch."

2 Divide the board into two sections. Cover the right side with craft paper in a contrasting color (letting a little bit of the background paper show around the edges). Cover a smaller section on the left (about 18 by 30 inches) with contrasting craft paper as well.

3 Post a copy of the Weather Graph on the left side. (See page 62.) Next to the graph add an open pocket notebook, placing strips of paper on the left (label this pocket "Blank Strips") and weather words on the right. (Label the top of this section "Weather Words." At the bottom, write "Add some of your own!") Above both, add a small sign that says "Weather Watcher." Use straight pins to hold strips of chart paper on which you can write children's names.

4 Next to the graph and pocket folder, display a child-size figure. (Invite a small child to lie down on a large sheet of craft paper. Have children trace around the child. Cut it out and decorate. (Children might even like to give this classmate a name.)

5 Make clothes for your board child to wear—including outfits for all kinds of weather. Display them on the right along with pushpins.

6 Bring children together to talk about the weather. Ask: "What was it like on the way to school today? Has anyone heard a prediction for later today or tomorrow?" Draw a picture on the graph to represent the weather. Write weather words on strips and place them in the pocket.

7 Invite children to dress the child on the board for the weather. Children can also do this on their own, using the clothes provided (and adding ones they make too) to show what they know about the day's weather.

SEASONAL AND HOLIDAY LINKS

 Make new clothes for the board to correspond with seasons and/or holidays. (Costumes in October will be a hit.) Invite children to add to the wardrobe too. Combine with discussions on how children's dress changes with the weather, the seasons, and the holidays.

Variations

Surprise Graphs: To keep interest high and strengthen science process skills, post surprise weather questions that invite children to graph predictions—and watch the weather to see what happens. Make up several graphs ahead of time so that you can easily change the graph. Questions might include "Will it rain today? Will the temperature go below freezing today? Will today be warmer than yesterday? Will it rain more than an inch this week?" Students can record predictions by writing their names on sticky notes and placing them next to Yes and No on the graph. Encourage children to discuss the reasoning behind their predictions and to investigate the answers.

Close-Up on Temperature: The reproducible graph lets children compare weather conditions over a period of time. Help them learn more about weather patterns by graphing temperature only. Hang an outdoor thermometer in an easy-to-read place. Make a graph to record the temperature each day. (Try to check it at the same time each day.) Have children use the information on the graph to make predictions. Ask, for example, "Do you think it will be warmer or colder tomorrow? Is the temperature warming up, cooling off, or staying about the same? Do you think you'll need a jacket tomorrow?" Over a period of a month or so, children may observe patterns in the weather.

Cloud Detectives: Pin a sheet of dark blue paper to the left side of the board. Divide it into five sections, one for each day of the school week. Have Weather Watchers draw a picture of the clouds each day (pastels will work well for this), adding sun or precipitation too if either is present. Guide children in making connections between types of clouds and weather conditions. For example, students will notice that on days when white, fluffy clouds (cumulus) are present, so is the sun. (The same is true for cirrus clouds (white, whispy clouds). When clouds are dark and low (cumulonimbus or stratus), rain may be falling or on the way. Encourage children to make predictions about the weather based on the clouds they see.

Teaching With the Board

A weather board will provide endless learning opportunities. A few suggestions follow:

Sun Stories: Share *Sun Song* by Jean Marzollo (HarperCollins, 1995), a lyrical story of the sun's activities from sunrise to sunset. Reread the story and have children listen for words that describe the sun's activities—for example, "call the sheep" and "kiss the face of a child."

> **The Sun** ☀
> dries up puddles
> makes me sweaty
> melts snow
> helps plants grow

Follow up by posting fresh paper at the bulletin board for listing children's own descriptions of the sun's activities.

Puddle Science: Children and puddles seem to go together. Take advantage of this connection to introduce evaporation. Set up a "Puddle Watch" on the left side of the board. If you don't have a real puddle outside to watch, make one in the classroom by pouring water into a shallow pan. Have children measure the puddle and draw a picture of it (outline only) on the board. Each day (or if it's particularly sunny and warm, several times a day), take a new measurement. Have children draw the outline of the puddle each time. Ask: "What is happening to the puddle?" Learn more by reading *Where Do Puddles Go?* by Fay Robinson (Children's Press, 1995), a Rookie Read-About-Science book.

Symbols Tell Stories: With the Weather Watch bulletin board, your students have been using pictures to convey information—pictures of the sun, clouds, and so on—that shows what kind of day it is. Introduce weather reports in the newspaper, complete with maps. (Children can bring these in from home and share them.) Together, look for symbols. Have children suggest possible meanings for the symbols before explaining, if need be, what they mean. Use the maps and symbols to look at weather in other parts of the country and make comparisons.

Weather Graph

Fun With a Friend

This board brings children together in collaborative activities, encouraging the partnerships and cooperation that help create a caring and supportive atmosphere in your classroom.

LEARNING LINKS

You can use this board all year to support learning goals, changing the directions to meet your needs. The board pictured invites children to look at themselves and at a friend and draw what they see, encouraging attention to detail, eye-hand coordination, social skills, and more. For more ideas, see Variations, page 64.

Building the Board

Steps

1 Cover the board with craft paper and add a border.

2 Display a sign: "Fun With a Friend." Add a smaller sign beneath this that says "I will look at me and draw what I see. I will look at you and draw you too!"

Materials

⊙ craft paper

⊙ mirror

⊙ hammer and nails

⊙ spring-type clips

⊙ drawing paper pad

⊙ crayons or markers

3 Affix a mirror securely to the board. You will be able to hammer a picture framing hook or a nail through most bulletin boards and into the wall behind them.

4 Use nails or pins to attach two spring clips to the board next to the mirror. Space them to hold a pad of drawing paper. Place the pad of paper in the clips. Pin up an open box of crayons or markers. The multicultural sets work well for this activity.

5 Invite a pair of children to demonstrate the activity. Have one child look in the mirror and draw a self-portrait. Have that child then look at his or her partner and draw that child too. Encourage children to notice the kinds of details that will enhance their drawings—hair and eye color, the shape of a smile, and so on. The second child can then choose another child from the class and repeat the process. Children can continue, taking turns as both models and portrait artists.

SEASONAL AND HOLIDAY LINKS

 Plan activities to correspond with seasonal and holiday events within your school and community. For example, if your class or school gardens in the spring, set up a seed-sorting activity at the board. Glue or tape an assortment of seeds to index cards (one kind of seed per card). Form two large yarn circles on the board. Glue pieces of Velcro to the backs of the cards and to the board (inside the circles). Let children work in pairs to sort the seeds. (One can start each set and the other can try to guess the rule and continue sorting, or they can work together.) Holidays such as Halloween and Valentine's Day present similar opportunities.

Variations

Good Foods:

For a health and nutrition tie-in, change the display to picture two children. On one, write "I am happy, feeling good, because I eat healthy food." On the other, write "I'm not happy, feeling bad, junk food is all I had." Have children cut out pictures of different kinds of foods and pin them around the board. They can also add clean food containers to the display, such as an empty French fry box, an empty juice box, a candy bar wrapper, and a small milk carton. Let children visit the display in pairs, sorting the foods by placing them on one or the other picture. This display will grow and change as often as children add new items to it, inviting repeat visits.

Animals at Home: Change the display to explore animal habitats. Add pictures that show animal habitats on one side of the display. Put up pictures of animals on the other. (Children can cut these out of magazines or draw them.) Have children visit the board in pairs, working together to place animals in their habitats. Using removeable wall adhesive will allow them to easily move the animals from one place to another.

Team Tic-Tac-Toe: This variation of tic-tac-toe, from *About Teaching Mathematics* by Marilyn Burns (Math Solutions, 1992), will stretch your students' logical reasoning skills every time they play. Set up the board by changing the sign to read "Team up for Tic-Tac-Toe." Clip a fresh drawing pad to the board, and add a smaller pad of paper for students to record and post tips and to keep track of wins and losses. Post directions and a sample game board as follows for students who are new to the game:

⊙ Take turns placing an X or an O in one square on the board.

⊙ In regular tic-tac-toe, you have to stick with either Xs or Os. In this game, you can put down either an X or an O on each turn.

⊙ Try to be the first to get three in a row across, down, or diagonally.

Project Place

Students help themselves to the activities at this board—picking them up and taking them away to explore independently, in pairs, or in groups. You can plan the activities to focus on literature, science, theme studies, and more.

BORDER BOX

A simple scalloped border frames the display pictured here. For a student-built border, create a pattern with pictures of scissors, paper, glue, and felt pens.

LEARNING LINKS

Giving students a choice in how and what they learn is an important part of any curriculum. This board integrates choice, letting students choose from a variety of projects that reflect different learning styles. At the same time, the activities can reinforce whatever curriculum focus you choose.

Building the Board

Steps

1 Cover the board with craft paper and add a sign that says "Project Place." Add a second and smaller sign that indicates the content area, such as "Readers Workshop."

2 Pin or staple envelopes horizontally to hold standard-size reproducibles. Stock envelopes with assorted projects. Aim for variety in content and learning style—including some that invite children to express themselves artistically, some that involve building, creative writing, and so

Materials

- craft paper
- large manila envelopes
- assorted projects (see samples, pages 67–69)

66

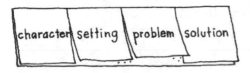

on. The ideas here will support a board with a language arts focus.

- **Using the Reproducibles:** Use page 70 to make flap books. Have children cut on the dashed lines, then fold in half on the solid line. They can use each flap page to tell something about the story. Use page 71 to make bookmarks featuring favorite characters.

- **Pocket Postcards:** Place large index cards for making postcards in a pocket. Children can write to a character in a book, from one character to another, or to a friend (telling about the book). The picture side can feature the setting of the story, an event, a character, and so on. Be sure to glue examples of both the front and back of sample postcards on the pocket for reference.

- **Accordion Books:** Children love these foldout books, which are easy to make and fun to write and illustrate. Let children make them to retell stories or to tell about stories they've read (title, author, characters, setting, and so on). Stock the pocket with precut strips of paper, post directions on the outside, and display a sample. (See page 7 for directions.)

 Set aside space for children to display some of their completed projects. Rotate frequently to shine the spotlight on all students.

SEASONAL AND HOLIDAY LINKS

Give the board added appeal from month to month by letting children "landscape" it to show changes in the world around them. Also set aside a spot for a Surprise Project—an activity you add to the board each month to reflect a holiday or other special event. For example, stock a Valentine's Day pocket with doilies, special paper cut to card size, new markers, and so on. Add a book for more fun. *Valentine Cats* by Jean Marzollo (Scholastic, 1996) is a perfect choice. (These cats cut out cards, write messages, add glitter and paint—inspiring your students to do the same.) Children will look forward to seeing what's inside this project pocket all year.

TIP

 For additional literature-based activities, try these resources:

- Better Than Book Reports *by Christine Boardman Moen (Scholastic Professional Books, 1992)*
- Easy Bookmaking *by Natalie Walsh (Scholastic Professional Books, 1996)*

Variations

Science Project Place: For a Project Place board with a science focus, look for activities that reinforce process skills. Plan them to support a particular unit of study or offer an assortment, building on previous as well as current topics. (Don't worry about covering old material. Revisiting concepts allows children to rethink ideas and build on what they know.) Examples of projects you might include to enrich a unit on plants include:

- **Shape Books:** Provide templates for making vegetable or fruit shape books.

- **Patterns in Nature:** Include patterns children can complete to show the way leaves grow on stems. (Look at various stems to see the different patterns.)

- **Sorting and Graphing:** Provide seeds to sort and graph. (Include string circles to sort seeds into, a journal page to record sorting methods, and simple graphs children can fill in by drawing pictures to graph seeds by color, size, texture, and so on.)

- **Book Break:** Offer a book about plants (fiction or nonfiction) and a response sheet.

- **Word Builders:** Make up vocabulary-building activity sheets that invite children to observe a plant or plant part in detail and write as many descriptive words as they can For example, write "lima bean seed" at the top and provide simple directions. Children might respond by writing the words *hard, curved, smooth, off-white.*

- **Poetry Connection:** Share plant poetry, such as "Green With Envy" by Eve Merriam (from *The Earth Is Painted Green*; Scholastic, 1994), and provide a blank book for students to add their own poems to (these might be other poems they find or poems they write).

Math Project Place: From problem-solving to sorting activities, there are many ways to stock your Project Place pockets to strengthen math skills. Examples follow.

- **Scavenger Hunt:** To reinforce measurement skills, divide a sheet of paper into six or eight squares and write a measurement in each (for example, 1-inch long, 1-foot high, 2-feet around, and so on). Challenge children to find something in the room that is about the same size as each measurement listed. Have them use words or pictures to record the names of objects they find.

- **Problem-Solving With Shapes:** Make copies of the shape reproducible on page 25 for an activity that invites children to problem-solve with shapes. Cut out the shapes and use them to create a design on a piece of paper. Trace around the outer edge of the design, remove the shapes, and make copies. Place designs and shapes (stored in resealable bags) in the pocket. Have children fill in the designs without overlapping any shapes or going outside the outline. After students have tried this activity once, they can add their own outlines to the activity pocket for classmates to complete.

- ⊙ **Literature-Based Math:** You can find a children's book to reinforce just about any math concept. *The Doorbell Rang* by Pat Hutchins (Greenwillow, 1986) is a favorite with children. In this story, two children figure out how to share cookies among themselves, then readjust their solutions as more and more people stop by. Place a copy of the story in a Project Place pocket along with small paper plates (or 6-inch construction paper circles) and small circles that represent cookies. Write story-based problems on paper for children to solve—for example, "Share 12 cookies equally between two people, three, four, and so on." Have children place cookies on plates to indicate their answers. *Literature-Based Math Activities* by Alison Abrams (Scholastic Professional Books, 1992) is a good resource for more ideas.

- ⊙ **Roll It:** A pair of dice in a pocket along with a list of activities will reinforce probability and statistics. Sample activities include recording the number of tries it takes to roll a 1 (try five times), a 6 (compare with rolls to get a 1), and so on; rolling two dice as many times as you can without getting doubles (keep a running record in the pocket to see who sets the record); rolling two dice, keeping a running total. How many rolls to get to 100? (Based on material in *About Teaching Mathematics* by Marilyn Burns; Math Solutions, 1992.)

Flap Book

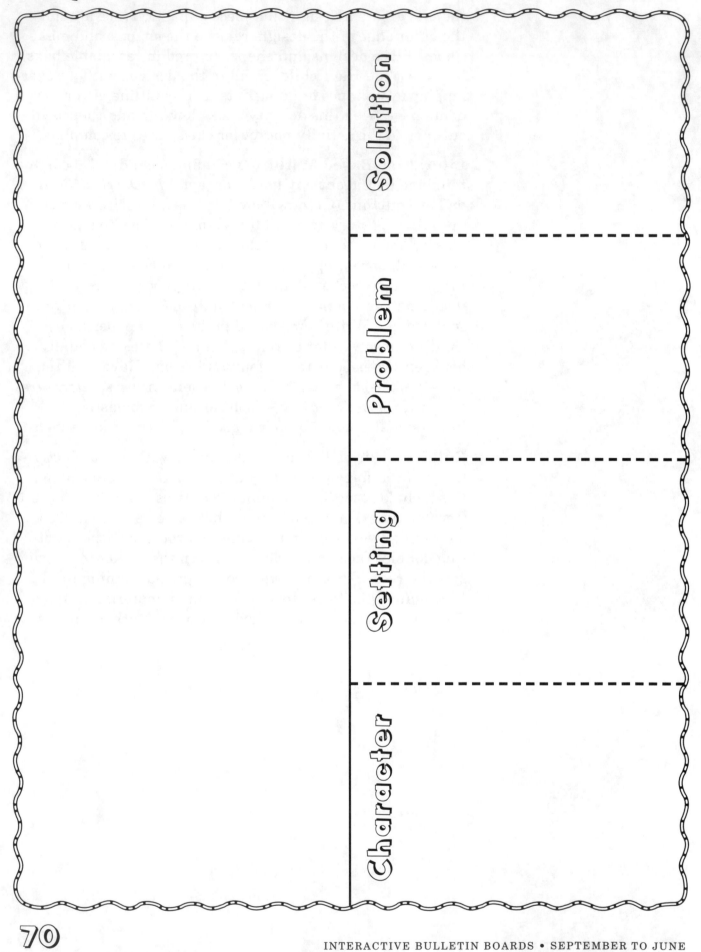

Solution

Problem

Setting

Character

Make a Bookmark

1. Cut on the - - - - - - - - - lines.
2. Fold on the _____ line. Put glue on the inside.
   Press both sides together.
3. Draw a picture of a character's face. Paste it to the top
   of your bookmark.
4. Complete both sides of the bookmark.

Title

_____

_____

Author

_____

_____

Illustrator

_____

_____

My favorite character

_____

_____

The best part of this
story

_____

_____

_____

Something I learned
from this story

_____

_____

_____

INTERACTIVE BULLETIN BOARDS • SEPTEMBER TO JUNE
Scholastic Professional Books, 1998

Try to Paint Like...

This board will inspire children to try out the styles of some of the world's most famous artists—from Sonia Delaunay to Diego Rivera—and discover their own artistic talents in the process. Its simple setup makes it easy to keep fresh all year long, introducing students to a new artist each month.

LEARNING LINKS

Creative expression is at the heart of every child. This board nurtures children's aesthetic development, encouraging them to experiment with different media and techniques and promoting positive attitudes toward art.

Building the Board

Steps

Materials

- craft paper
- assorted art prints
- pushpins
- spring clips
- assorted art paper
- paints, paintbrushes
- collage materials
- crayons, colored pencils

1 Schedule artists to feature at the display. Aim for variety in technique and style, time period, gender, and ethnicity. For suggestions, see Seasonal and Holiday Links.

2 Cover a board with craft paper and add a sign that says "Try to paint like…" Add the name of your featured artist and display a poster and other examples of his or her work.

TIP

 Museums are a good source of art prints and postcards. Additional resources are Exploring Masterpieces With Young Learners *by Rhonda Graff Silver (Scholastic Professional Books, 1996), with four full-color reproductions, and* Month-by-Month Masterpieces *(Scholastic Professional Books, 1996), with full-color reproductions of 10 masterpieces.*

3 Use pushpins to attach spring clips to the board. Clip a fresh piece of paper in place and let a young artist go to work. Keep a supply of art materials and papers nearby. A small desk can hold paints and other materials as students work.

4 Have children display their work around the board. When it's time to change the featured artist, have children place their artwork in portfolios. (Tape two large pieces of oaktag together along both sides and the bottom to make a simple portfolio.) At the end of the year they'll have their own collections of fine art to share with families! (Be sure to pull portfolios out periodically to share at open school night and parent conferences.)

SEASONAL AND HOLIDAY LINKS

 Look for artists whose work captures the feel of a season—for example, Monet's *Spring* or Utagawa Hiroshige's *Sudden Shower on the Ohashi Bridge* (for rainy times). Or feature artists by birthday months—for example, Louise Nevelson in September, Georgia O'Keefe in November, and Paul Klee in December.

Variations ∙ ∘ ∙ ∘ ∙ ∘ ∙ ∘ ∙ ∘ ∙ ∘ ∙ ∘ ∙ ∘ ∙ ∘ ∙ ∘ ∙ ∘ ∙ ∘ ∙ ∘ ∙ ∘ ∙ ∘ ∙ ∘ ∙ ∘

Through the Window: Look for artists whose work will inspire parallel work by students. For example, Marc Chagall's *Paris Through the Window* can inspire students' own paintings of what they see out their windows. Edwin Landseer's *Dignity and Impudence*, a painting of a large and small dog side by side, can inspire students' paintings of large and small comparisons. Children can respond to Van Gogh's *Bedroom at Arles* with paintings of their own bedrooms.

Meet the Illustrators: Substitute favorite children's illustrators in place of famous artists. Time your choices to correspond with author studies or, like the Happy Birthday board, with birthday months. Place a book featuring the illustrator's work on a music stand next to the board. Display other samples of the illustrator's work on the board. (Contact publishers for biographical and other material.) Clip fresh paper to the board and let children experiment with the illustrator's style, colors, and so on. A sampling of favorite illustrators follows:

⊙ **Kevin Henkes:** Whimsical watercolors capture characters' personalities in *Lilly's Purple Plastic Purse* (Greenwillow, 1996) and the other charming mouse books (*Owen, Chrysanthemum, Julius, Baby of the World, Chester's Way, Sheila Rae, The Brave, A Weekend With Wendell*) and will inspire students to illustrate new tales about these friends.

⊙ **J. Brian Pinkney:** This illustrator sometimes works in scratchboard, as he did for *The Boy and the Ghost* (Simon & Schuster, 1989). Students can experiment with this technique by putting a layer of black crayon on paper and scratching away to create a picture or design. (Pinkney uses black ink on illustration board.)

⊙ **Peggy Rathman:** Vibrant colors and humorous details characterize this illustrator's work, including the Caldecott-winning *Officer Buckle and Gloria* (Putnam, 1995). Children will have fun trying to capture this quality in their own paintings. The classroom will be a great source of ideas. What kinds of humorous things happen here every day?

⊙ **Lois Ehlert:** The collage artwork in *Growing Vegetable Soup* (Scholastic, 1987), *Chicka Chicka Boom Boom* (Simon & Schuster, 1989), and other books illustrated by Ehlert features bold shapes and colors that children will love experimenting with themselves.

Teaching With the Board

Use art to integrate your curriculum. Suggestions follow.

About the Artist: Set up an area next to the display to hold items related to the artist that children bring in from home. These might include a postcard with the artist's work on it, a color, a pattern, an object, and so on. Provide sticky notes so that children can explain the connection between the item and the artist.

Poetry and Paintings: Use the art of Tao-Chi to integrate poetry and painting. Tao-Chi, a Chinese artist, used bamboo brushes and ink to create expressive interpretations of nature. In the Chinese tradition, these paintings combined calligraphy, poetry, and painting. Share prints of Tao-Chi's work. Then let children create their own ink paintings, complete with poetry and fancy lettering. (Children might compose their own poems or copy favorite poems from books.) Share these tips to enhance children's work:

⊙ To achieve light and dark tones in your work, use ink in different strengths, watering some down to create varying shades.

⊙ Use scroll-shaped paper for the full effect.

⊙ Experiment with brush strokes to achieve different effects. Try pulling, pushing, and twirling the brush. Use brushes of different thicknesses to make thick and thin lines.

Color Engineers: Clothing catalogs are a great source of unusual colors and names. Set small groups of children up with cups of primary-color paints, craft sticks, and paper plates. Have them experiment with mixing colors on the plates, using the craft sticks like palette knives. What new colors can they create? Have them record color equations on copies of page 76 to show combinations. Display and discuss. Where do students draw inspiration from in naming their colors? (For example green fruits and vegetables might inspire paint colors called celery, kiwi, and dill pickle.)

Color Engineers

Mix colors together to make new colors. Paint a sample of each in the spaces to make color equations. Make up names for your new colors.

Color 1		Color 2		Color 3	My New Color's Name
_____	+	_____	=	_____	_____
_____	+	_____	=	_____	_____
_____	+	_____	=	_____	_____
_____	+	_____	=	_____	_____
_____	+	_____	=	_____	_____

Try mixing more than two colors together to make new colors. Use the back of this paper to write your equations.

INTERACTIVE BULLETIN BOARDS • SEPTEMBER TO JUNE
Scholastic Professional Books, 1998

Snapshots

Ideas for seven more interactive bulletin boards follow.

Puzzle Map

Students love puzzles with giant pieces, and with this board they get a year's worth. With a focus on the United States, this board familiarizes students with the names and shapes of states and stimulates their interest in geography. Students sign up in teams for states they will feature on the puzzle board. After enlarging an outline of the state, they trace it on the board

and then cut the puzzle into pieces and place them in a box tacked to the board. Students can visit the board in small groups to put the puzzle together, then add information about the state—for example, pictures showing the state flower and bird, natural resources, bodies of water, landmarks, and so on. When it's time to put up a new puzzle, place puzzle pieces coming down into a large resealable bag and store in a box near the board. Students can put puzzles together on the floor as a free-time activity.

Watch This Space

For a schoolwide board, try this favorite. Cover a display space in a hallway or in the media center with dark craft paper. Add a sign that says "Watch This Space." Invite classes to sign up by the week. During their allotted time they can add pictures and information to the board. As children watch the board develop, they will be guided in the direction they take. Young children might start the board, adding pictures of the sun, moon, and stars and interesting facts about each. As older children take a turn, they can add more detail—for example, adding planets along with informative captions. Students will be drawn to the board all year as each class adds new information and pictures.

Recycle It

You'd be amazed at what children can do with a bunch of boxes—or any other recycled material. Newspapers become cities, scrap paper becomes abstract art. To get this board going, just cover a wall space for students. Then have them decide on an idea (such as Paper City, Box-Lid Building, or The Paper Connection) and let them begin. They'll soon fill the board, developing their idea as they go. To give each child input in the decision-making process, form committees of children and let each be responsible for the start of a new recycling board.

Look What Kids Can Do

This board puts students in charge of displaying their art. Just cover a board, add a sign ("Look What Kids Can Do") and an "Exhibitor" sign-up sheet, and let children add art as they wish. This board presents a good opportunity to discuss appropriate responses to others' work. Ask: "How can you tell if something you say about a picture on the board is appropriate?" (Encourage children to recognize that if they ask themselves if anyone's feelings could be hurt and the answer is yes, they need to keep the thought to themselves.) Help children recognize ways to make positive comments about their own and others' work by modeling responses. For example, you might notice the vibrant colors in one child's art, the happy faces on another child's people (you might ask why they are smiling), the many shapes in a geometric design. By focusing on process, not product, you can help children appreciate their own and others' efforts.

Fabulous Frames

These frames are a favorite with teachers and students. Make a frame for every four to five students by cutting out the center of a piece of oaktag, leaving a couple of inches all the way around. Tack the frame to the board on both sides and the top. Leave the bottom open to make it easy to slip pictures in and out. Write students' names on cards and post next to the frames. Thread a ribbon through a star and the card (staple in place at both ends of the card) so that children can move the star up and down to indicate the current exhibitor. Children who have artwork that is smaller than the opening can mount it on larger paper to fit.

Creativity Corner

Stock a shelf or worktable near a bulletin board with art supplies, such as collage materials, colored pencils, markers, scissors, glue, recyclables, and so on. Cover the board with craft paper and add a sign that says "Creativity Corner" or "Our Classroom Gallery." Let children visit the area to create and display works of art. Add a sign-in sheet that says "Now showing the work of…." Let children sign their names to the sheet when they display work. Look for an unused corner of your room for this display. Children can get messy with materials without interfering with what's happening in other parts of the room and their work will brighten up an otherwise neglected space.

Friendly Faces Border

This child-made border frames your classroom, bringing together all of your wall displays with a ring of friendly faces. Just have children each paint or color pictures of themselves. (Have them all use the same size paper to help unify elements in the border.) Children can do as many of these as they want to go all the way around the room. Display along the top edges of each wall. Save some from each year to start off the next. This will not only help make young children feel at home but it will let them know how much you value your students' work.